How To Get Everything Out Of Life

If You Can Count to Four...

Excerpts from the works of **Dr. J. B. Jones** and **Earl Shoaff**

edited by **Dr. Robert C. Worstell**

Get Related Materials
from Our Free Library
Instant Access – Join Here

Click or type into your browser:

http://livesensical.com/go/freelibrary/

Authors:

John Earl Shoaff (1916-1965)

Dr. J. B. Jones (1917-1987?)

About this work:

The first half is a transcript derived from Shoaff's only known surviving speech, given in 1962. No copyright renewal found on record.

The second half is excerpted as fair use from the first chapter of Jones' bestseller "If You Can Count to Four...", published in 1957, no copyright renewal found on record.

Note: Spellings and grammar have been retained from the originals, to remain with the writers' and transcriber's intent.

How to Get Everything You Want - 1

"How To Get Everything You Want Out Of Life"

I just want to take a few moments and cover some things that have assisted me in acquiring things in my life.

I know that few people are aware of these basic fundamental laws that operate in this world of ours. Some people are aware of them; some people are not aware of them, but they are using them. And sometimes we wonder why certain things happen to us, we acquire certain things and then over a period of time it seems like we live in stagnation. Nothing happens; nothing takes place; everything seems to be at a standstill.

There are basic laws in this universe that we are governed by and will work for you if you know how to apply them. And I would like to cover a couple of these laws that will assist you in knowing why these things happen.

For an example, everybody is aware of the law of gravitation. Now, we don't know how it works, but we know it works. It works for everybody. It doesn't matter whether you are a saint or whether you are the opposite of a saint. If you jumped off a 20-story building and you are a saint and you land on a concrete sidewalk, you are going to be an unhealthy saint. If you happen to be a crook and you do the same thing, the same thing happens to you. So basically, it doesn't matter if you are good or bad--if you use the law of gravity wrong you are going to suffer.

The law of electricity works for all of us. If we use it properly, we can light our homes by screwing a light bulb into a socket. If we stick our finger into it, then we get bit. You're going to get burned. We can burn your house down with electricity or you can light your home with it. You can cook with it. You can use refrigeration--all the great things

How to Get Everything You Want - 2

that electricity will do for us!

You do not have to be an electrical-minded person. You don't have to be a genius to do it. A child three years old can push a button and turn the lights on. And one of the greatest electrical engineers in the world, all he can do when he pushes that button is that he can turn the lights on, too. So basically, it does not matter. It will work for you. We have laws to success.

We have laws of poverty. We have laws of lack, laws of prosperity. We have laws of hate. We have laws of love. We have laws of peace. All of these are basic laws. If we use them rightfully, wonderful things will happen to us. If we use them wrong, then we get ourselves in trouble.

Now, one of the things that has always bothered me, in all the books I've ever read on setting goals in life, positive thinking, positive goals in life--many of you have probably read some of the books--you follow these different steps, rules, laws, that if we set 10 goals we end up with 2. We lose out on 8. So it is not like the law of gravity seemingly, because it doesn't work every time. And one of the reasons it does not work every time, is that we do not use the right law. We are using part of the law, and so the law of averages will give you a percentage of your goals. That is all.

You say, "Gee, wasn't that great? It happened to me." But whatever happened to all the other goals you had in life?

I'm going to lay down a simple basic way and you can have anything material you want to have and you can be anything you want to be, and it's a simple basic situation. There's absolutely no problem to it. These are scientific things that work every time if you will do it in a simple way.

Now, the first thing we want to become aware of is we want to be like farmers. We are going to plant seeds, and

How to Get Everything You Want - 3

these seeds that we plant are the seeds that we're going to reap. Now we're all aware that if we plant a seed of tomatoes, we are not going to get cucumbers--we're going to get tomatoes. If you plant a watermelon seed, you're not going to get grapefruit. You're not going to get radishes. If you want radishes, folks, you're going to have to plant radish seeds. And when you plant a seed in the earth, you must plant it properly. If you do not plant it properly, you will not have the harvest. One of the major problems in our country today for the average person is they take the time and the effort to buy all the harvesting equipment, but they do not understand the planting and the cultivating.

We want to reap harvest, but we do not want to take the time to plant, and we do not want to take the time to cultivate. Now the planting of the seeds in the earth is basically and absolutely the same process that you use in the mental world.

We are born with a conscious mind and a sub-conscious mind. We are the only animal in the kingdom that have both the conscious and the sub-conscious mind--a mind that can decide anytime in life where we want to go or what we want or what we don't want. We can decide with this accomplished mind of ours if we want to do a thing or if we don't want to do a thing. We can decide if we want to eat or if we don't want to eat. We can decide if we want a drink, or if we don't want a drink. We can decide what we want in life in a home, in an automobile, in the clothes we wear, anything that we want in this world--any type of furniture, any type of a home, any type of an anything.

We decide at anytime. Now, where most people are making mistakes is that they simply set their goals down. Now, what are your goals? Write them down. A fellow says, I want a house, a car, some furniture, I want some money. And this is the way they set their goals.

How to Get Everything You Want - 4

Now he has a whole group of seeds, let's say apple seeds. We had 50 different types of apple seeds, and we just grabbed any of those seeds and we throw them in the ground and they come up and they're green apples. I wanted red ones. That's because you picked any type of an apple seed. You didn't describe it. So we must learn to define.

Now, you've heard of the word "visualizing". You have to learn to visualize things. And when you visualize something, this is the thing that's going to come in your life, if the visualization is strong enough. Now we're always visualizing things in our life, but the tendency is to visualize negative situations. Now the reason that we're visualizing negative situations in our life is because, let's not kid ourselves, we're living in a negative world.

So if I say, "Joe, how are you feeling today?" And he says, "Good, fine." And I ask him the next day how he feels, and he says, "I feel terrible. I've got a pain in my stomach and I ache all over." And he goes into a...you'd think he was an actor. He can describe a negative situation in his body so wonderfully. But when he feels good, he just says, "Fine." How come people, when they feel fine, they don't say, "I feel great; I feel wonderful; I feel so great that I expect all the wonderful things in the world to happen to me today!"?

In other words, have a little feeling when you talk about the good things in life. I say, "How are you doing in business?" You say, "Fine." Now if he has a bad day, he says when I ask him about his day, "Lousy, let me tell you this is a...I'm just having a terrible time. Did you read that article the other day? It took me several hours to find it; it was on the back page down at the bottom in fine print, but I located it."

People love negative things. They seem to vibrate with them. For some strange reason, they don't want things

How to Get Everything You Want - 5

that are negative in their life, but they keep insisting on talking about them. And they can paint the most beautiful picture of lost and lack.

I say by the way, "Internal..." and everybody immediately starts shaking..."combustion." A guy says, "You know what I thought you were going to say?" And he starts creating pictures and he says, by the way, I wonder about last year, what I did with that...I wonder if they'll find that...and immediately he says, I can see the guy coming in the door now...I wonder when he'll be here...I wonder what he'll look like... and he gets beautiful pictures, and the next thing you know, the guy is knocking on his door. He created the picture and he brought it into his life.

And the funny thing about creating things, folks: we are creators. Nothing comes to us. Everything comes through us from us. Everything in this world that happens to us comes from here, not out here.

And everything that you have in your life is exactly what you designed, the dress you're wearing, the coat you're wearing, the tie you're wearing, the necklace you're wearing, the home you're living in, the neighbors you've got, the friends you've got and the Senators you've got.

So don't blame me for people that you attracted! When you signed this person up, you're the guy that coached them in. You didn't care who it was as long as he came in. And pretty soon, you helped plenty of them and you say, "You know what, Shoaff? I've got a lousy bunch of distributors."

Well, when you understand these laws, you won't tell me these things. I'm not talking about you, or you--I wouldn't dare. There's too many here. What I am saying is that everything we attract is what we are, and what I am speaks so loudly I can't hear what you say. And what you are speaks so loudly I cannot hear what you say. So

How to Get Everything You Want - 6

everything you say is the thing that you created. So be careful what you create. Be careful. It's hard to visualize a thing.

Let's try something, folks. Let's visualize a 707, shall we? What's a 707 look like? I've only been in one a couple of times. I've only seen one in the air once. It's hard to visualize one. You want to visualize an automobile, or a stole? I don't know why I keep saying "stole."

My wife must be visualizing a stole. I keep getting that feeling...every time we come to New York. You see, we have to learn how to describe things. Now I'm going to go through a description of a thing because this is very important in your life, folks. Please try to remember what I'm saying. You can change your life that quick. You can have everything wonderful in your life; you can have everything wonderful happening to you, if you use these few basic little things.

Now I'm going to describe a thing--an automobile. I'll talk about an automobile because an automobile is easy to describe, and people can comprehend it very quickly and very easily. I'm not going to talk about a Chevrolet; I'm going to talk about a Cadillac. Anytime I'm talking about a Cadillac, folks, I'm not describing the Cadillac per se; I'm talking about a Cadillac idea--the Cadillac idea in the clothing, in the home and the things you really desire deep within you. And I'm not talking about something that you say. "Well, I've got to have money to buy a Cadillac." I'm not talking about money. It's not necessary that you have money to have a Cadillac. There are many wonderful things that can happen to you. These things can come to you from many unusual sources. Many wonderful things can happen to you.

If you believe in the thing I'm talking about, your income can be doubled, tripled, quadrupled. The one thing that I had in my mind that I had defined in my mind was a red

How to Get Everything You Want - 7

Cadillac convertible. I never had owned a Cadillac in my life. Now you probably don't want a red Cadillac. I wanted one, and I defined that thing right down to the socks, and the end result was I had me a red Cadillac convertible, and my income increased to a point where it cost me nothing. This is visualizing. This is a positive attitude toward the things you want.

Too many people stop their dreams because they start thinking about that thing that is not necessary in order to have it. I say to somebody, "Do you want a new Cadillac?" You say, "I want one, but I can't afford it." I say, "It has nothing to do with affording. I just want to know what you really want."

Most people are afraid to define what they want in life. They're afraid it's going to cost them something. Well if you're making $1,000 a month right now, and you double your income to $2,000 per month, you can have a Cadillac, you can have two Cadillacs, you can have five Cadillacs. Don't worry about the income-- I'm just talking about the principle now. The Cadillac--what do you do about it? I'll say, "Pete, what would you like to have?" He says, "A Cadillac." Now don't forget folks, I'm going to give it to him--I'm going to give it to him. He has nothing to worry about--no money, no nothing. I say, "Pete, what do you want?" He says, "A Cadillac." I say, "Fine, Pete."

Now this is where people make their mistakes. I say, "I've got a nice 1936 beat-up model downstairs. I'll give it to you." He says, "I don't want a 1936 model Cadillac." I said, "You just told me you wanted a Cadillac." He says, "I want a '62 Cadillac." I said, "Why didn't you tell me, Pete? Why didn't you tell me?" This is the way people set their dreams. He doesn't just want a Cadillac. Do you want an orange or a green one? He says, "I want a red one."

Now he's starting to define. And you know it's very difficult to define up here in your mind. The first thing

How to Get Everything You Want - 8

you do is you get a piece of paper folks, and you start defining on a piece of paper. A 1962 Cadillac, a red Cadillac, a convertible--I'm just describing one car now. You can have any kind of car you want--a red Cadillac, 1962 convertible with a white top, red/white upholstery, a red floor, white wall tires, electric windows, a/c unit. The guy says, "How much does that cost?" I say, "Don't worry bout it--you're going to get it for nothing." The guy says, "I'll take it, then." Now he says, "I'm going to put everything down then." That's right--describe it right down to the tee.

And when he gets all through, the perfect visualization is up here now because he has described it. When you write it, you start seeing it. He gets the picture up here by writing it down here. This is how you define things that you want in this world. When he gets that Cadillac completely defined in his mind, he's got the seed. He hasn't planted it yet. He's got it picked out.

Now the important thing is that you must release that seed. You must release it and it must be planted. And the perfect thing in the world to plant that seed is to take this piece of paper now and write the concept, "Thank you". That's the law of acceptance. And you would be amazed how many people in this world can't accept their goods. You would be shocked. "Thank you" means you have accepted it. "I'm going to have it. I know it's mine." Then you take and you fold this piece of paper up with this goal on it, with this dream, with this desire and you put it away--put it underneath a tablecloth some place, put it in a drawer some place. Don't carry it around and don't take it out and look at it anymore. When you do this, that is planting it in the subconscious mind.

You've accepted--you've put it into the subconscious mind, and the thing starts to work. Now when you put this thing away, the reason you put it away after you have

How to Get Everything You Want - 9

defined it: the seed has been planted in the subconscious mind. You put it away some place, never to be looked at again. The reason for it is like planting a seed in the earth, folks. If you go and dig that seed up two or three times a day to look at it, nothing's going to happen.

If you've never seen a lack of faith--it's the farmer who had the gullibility to dig up the seed to see if it was growing yet. Now that is little faith. He really believes in the laws of growth, and that's the same way with us human beings. This is the way we're making our mistakes. When we plant in the subconscious mind, and it's there, the dream is there. The dream starts working towards you, the Cadillac starts working towards you, and events start taking place out here, and the next thing you know it's getting closer and closer to you.

Now if you take it out, and you start to look at it, the thing that happens is we say, "I wonder where it's coming from." This is a true showing of a lack of faith. "I wonder when it's coming. I wonder how it's coming." And so you are putting doubt in your law, and it will not come, folks. It will not come to you.

Now, what's going to happen to the seed that you planted in the subconscious mind: you'll be driving down the street, you'll be in a restaurant talking to a friend and all of a sudden, there's a red Cadillac convertible with a white top and the whole thing will hit you again and you'll see your dream. And it'll keep coming back.

The reason it'll keep coming back to you is this is the only way that the universal law has of talking to you. There's no voice--it's all in visualization. And when this dream comes up, what it really means is that's it's on its way to you. It is on its way to you--it's right around the corner. And so you do not at that time say, "How, when or where." All you do is say, "Thank you" because you know it's on its way. And then immediately put it back out of your mind.

How to Get Everything You Want - 10

And how would you act if you really and truly wanted a red Cadillac convertible--if you really and truly wanted one and it was a strong desire in your life, and you knew it was on its way, how would you act? You'd be excited, wouldn't you? You'd feel good--you'd say, "Man it's almost here, it's almost here." You'd walk taller, you'd look taller. You'd be happier. You'd be full of positive. You'd act different. Wonderful things are going to happen to you.

Where does the positive attitude come in at? It automatically creates a positive attitude because it's the law of expectancy. Good things are going to happen. You have planted your seeds properly, and they are working themselves to you, and you are automatically a positive person because all these wonderful things are going to happen. Don't just have one seed planted, folks--plant many seeds--any great desire you have in your life--a tangible object or intangible object. You can have anything in this world you want to have and you can be anything in this world you want to be by using this simple process.

There is absolutely no way you can keep success from your door, if you will just follow this basic, simple little process that I just described. This is the law of life, and every one of you people have worked this process. Maybe you weren't completely aware of how you worked it.

But think about it--that's why you only get 3 out of 8 things, or 1 out of 8 or 1 out of 10, because you didn't know exactly the process you were using. Now you know the process, so you can deal with anything in this world. Children--our children, folks. How many times have you heard people say to their children when the child says, "I'm going to be President of The United States," and the father and mother will say to them, "You? With your studies, you'll never make it, Junior." Now this is a wonderful seed to plant in that fertile little brain. The

How to Get Everything You Want - 11

subconscious is putting in the mind--telling him he can't; he's not smart enough.

The child says, "I'm going to be a rich man when I grow up. I'm going to have everything in this world." You say, "You? You're going to have to learn a lot, junior. You don't know how to handle money. You've got to learn how to use that ol' elbow grease." Anybody who's ever used much elbow grease, if he's ever made millions, I'll assure you the elbow grease is up here.

Now, what do you want to tell Junior? Anytime any children come to you or to their parents, you should tell your children, "Junior, you're the type of child who can have anything in this world. You have the ability and the intelligence to go anywhere, do anything and have everything in this world.

It is yours because you're that type of a child. Start planting these seeds in our children. This country today is teaching too many children, too many children, what to think instead of how to think.

And what are we? We are only children a little older than the other children. We are grown-up children, and we have to at some time in life, we have to start deciding and pinpointing things that we want in this world. And I'm not just talking about the tangible objects. I'm talking about intangible things.

What would you like to be? What type of person would you like to be? Would you like to have more love in your life? Well then, you must learn to give love. You'll never have anything without giving. Everything I have I receive back, multiplied. If I have a lot of hate in my life, I'm giving a lot of hate out.

And so if I don't want hate coming in my life, I shouldn't be giving it out. If I don't want people to talk about me, I shouldn't be talking about people. Everything that I send

How to Get Everything You Want - 12

out, I get back with feeling. Every thought I think I don't get, because I didn't plant my seed properly--I did not have a true visualization.

How many of you ladies have thought of a beautiful dress or a beautiful something that you don't have. How many would love to have a mink stole? A few years ago, if my wife even mentioned a mink stole, the first thing that would come in my mind was, "Where are you going to get it from? How are you going to pay for it?" I did not understand these things. When you just say, "mink stole," do you know what?

I never was aware that there was so many mink stoles in this country--every kind of every price and color and designs and everything else, and if you don't even know the exact kind you want, how do you know if you can ever expect to have it? Do you know the amazing thing? The average person in this world, and I'm only saying this because we are the average people of the world, and I say average because I am talking to an intelligent group of people. I'm not talking to people way down the ladder. I'm talking to a group of intelligent people. And I'm saying this, and you analyze this yourself.

Ask yourself this basic question. Do you know what you want in life? If I were to ask you right now, "What do you really want? What is a tangible object that you want in this world--things you can feel and touch and smell?

What are the things you want in life?" And you know, folks, the amazing thing--I doubt if there's 2% of the people in this room who can tell me and describe it, and just like that come right out and say it. So, what is success in your life? What is it that you want? Define it. Write it down. Pinpoint every drop of that dream that you have in your mind. Define it so clearly on that piece of paper that you can completely see it in your mind. And when you get it written down, write "thank you" on it and plant that

How to Get Everything You Want - 13

seed and put it away, and it will start to materialize and it will start coming into your life.

That is anything folks, anything.

Now a guy says, "I'm going to put down The Statler Hotel." You know why it wouldn't work for him? I'm not saying it won't work for the fellow, but I am saying that it won't work for the average person. Do you know why? He couldn't even imagine getting it. He can write it down. He can define it, and he can put "thank you" on it, but he can never plant the seed.

And the reason he can't is because he couldn't even imagine getting The Statler Hotel, that's why. And don't forget, this is something you have to accept--you're going to have it, folks. I told people about a Cadillac, average people working on average jobs. I said, "Do you want a Cadillac?" The guys said, "No, no, I don't want no Cadillac." I said, "Well, why don't you want a Cadillac?" He said, "For one thing, it cost so much to operate them." You see, he doesn't want one--he isn't ready for that step yet.

Now see, he steps from one car to another to another. He raises his consciousness, until pretty soon, he can buy Cadillacs like the average person buys a pair of shoes. And you can grow; you can grow in your thinking. People say, "Boy, you got to be careful about people--they'll take you in if you're not careful." They get such a wonderful visualization--they're always getting taken in. So you see how we build these pictures in our mind? People will spend the morning; they're going to get ready for a wonderful day.

Tomorrow morning, we're getting ready for a wonderful day; we're going out and it's going to be the most exceptional day we've ever had in our entire lives. I said, "How are you going to start the morning? Exactly what

How to Get Everything You Want - 14

are you going to do?" He says, "Well, the first thing I'm going to do is go out on the porch." He's going through his morning now--he's going to go out on his porch and get his newspaper and read a little bit about positive thinking in the headlines.

And if he can't find it there, he'll look and look and look and look until he finds something that is really good and negative and then he'll tell his wife and describe it, and he says, "Guess what I found in the paper?" And he starts telling her about some wonderful divorce that's taken place in the paper and the kids committed suicide, and he'll go on with this and he'll say, "Just imagine that, imagine that!"

And he'll describe it, and the negativity will get started and the wife will get negative and he will get more negative and when he gets all through with breakfast now, he's in such a nasty mood that he doesn't even like his dog! And he's going out to face the world with a positive attitude.

Do you see how ridiculous it is folks--some of the ridiculous things we do in life and we wonder why success doesn't always come to us in the proportion we'd like to have it come to us?

Expect wonderful things. Be a creator of ideas.

Let's not be moons, the reflector of ideas. Let's be suns, let's be the creator of the light; let's be the creator of the ideas, because we all have a capacity--that guardian of the gate, as the conscious mind. This guardian can at any time let any thought through to the subconscious mind it wants--any thought at any time.

We are thinking human beings. We have the capacity to think of anything, anything in this world we can think of, but we do not have the capacity to think of nothing. Now you try to imagine what nothing is. Try to get a thought of

How to Get Everything You Want - 15

that--there is absolutely no way. So that means we are thinking human beings and there are thoughts flying through our mind continuously--a steady flow of thoughts all the time coming through the mind.

Now where do these thoughts come from? All of a sudden, you say, "Gee, that thought must have come out of the clear blue sky." You didn't think of it, and it might have been something you didn't even know about. And the thought comes through and you say, "Well, that's kind of ridiculous, isn't it? That couldn't happen to me." And so you throw that thought aside. And if it's a good thought, why not accept it? Stop and analyze it and accept it. And let them happen to you.

And these objects come through to you all the time. A negative thought comes through and you say, "Boy, that's a good and negative thought and you start thinking about it and pretty soon you get a frown on your face and you think about it a little bit more and you create a beautiful picture and all of a sudden you put that down in the subconscious and you think, "Boy, there's another bad thing that's going to happen to me."

Have you ever caught yourself thinking about something you didn't want to think about and you've been thinking about it for 5 minutes and all of a sudden you think, "What am I thinking about that nasty thing for?" We do it; we do it all the time, folks.

But we can stop now, any time we want, and we can change that thought and we can put in a good thought. If you don't want to think about oranges, change the thought and think about bananas, if you want. If you don't want to think about lack, change the thought and think about prosperity. If you don't want to think about hate, think about love.

If you don't want to think of anything negative, put a

How to Get Everything You Want - 16

positive idea in your head. You know what happens, you can analyze and you can just dream about it and everything else, and get all these seeds planted properly and have all these wonderful things happen. Get twenty wonderful seeds planted, get them written down. Define. Thank you. Plant them into the subconscious mind.

Put it away, and every time it comes back into the subconscious mind and the law saying it's on its way, you just say "Thank you". Don't analyze it because it's already planted. Just say "Thank you" and go on.

Have ten, fifteen, twenty, thirty of these wonderful seeds planted and folks, you'll walk on air. You'll have miracles happen in your life. And don't be afraid to do this. Your wife isn't in harmony with the wonderful things you want to happen to you; well, if the husband isn't in harmony or if the children are not, or your friends aren't, you don't have to show them.

Plant your seeds privately then, and put them away privately and plant them deep and all these wonderful things will happen and you'll say, "You know, one thing about that person, I don't know what happened to him, but man oh man, everything they touch turns to gold. And that's the reason. That's the reason, folks--the proper planting of your seeds.

It was a real pleasure being here with you.

Thank you very much.

How to Get Everything You Want - 17

If You Can Count to Four...

If you can count to four, you can learn a simple set of rules which will unlock the treasures of the universe in all its dimensions.

Millions of people have been taught to believe that the rules of success are indeed so very difficult and complicated that surely they could never learn them.

The average person is perfectly willing to accept the fact that several hundred families in most any community are successful. They, at the same time, know that there are hundreds of communities in our own country and, of course, and all the other countries too.

If they would stop and think for a moment, they would also know that when you add up the hundreds in each community, and then multiply by the thousands of communities all over the world, that it would add up to hundreds of thousands of people who are very successful.

For example, not long ago it was my pleasure to visit Mexico City. I was surprised to learn that there are approximately 10,000 millionaires in Mexico City. We hear of the millions of extremely poor people in the country of Mexico. But, at the same time, there are 10,000 millionaires in just one city in Mexico. How could there be that many rich people and millions of poor people unless there is a basic system of rules that 10,000 of them are using and the millions are not using? I too, wondered about these perplexing problems for many years.

I was born into a family of 14 children down in the hills of Tennessee and the first 18 years of my life I was what was considered a poor boy. I observed hundreds of families who obviously were not poor. They had poise, culture, a feeling of well-being, self-confidence, a measure of health, and they had plenty of money to express life abundantly. I wondered why my wonderful parents did not have those things in abundance too. I was stirred to investigate and find out, if possible, the answer to this problem.

I found out that anyone can be genuinely successful if he will learn the exact same "rules" that the successful people learned and use them.

To be genuinely successful, to me, is to enjoy a large measure of happiness, health and prosperity. It is a balanced type of life; Harmonious living with good physical health and also plenty of money.

So, it was my privilege to start out as a poor, unhappy person and to make the same observations that the millions are now making. It was my privilege to learn these basic rules and to take them out into the hard-boiled business world and to challenge every one of them. *And to discover, beyond any shadow of a doubt, that there not only is a system of rules, but that anyone, not just a few, can learn them and use them and become just as successful as he wants to be.*

The title of this section, "If You Can Count to Four" is designed to tell you that regardless of your background, your lack of education, your lack of knowing anyone who is supposed to be important, your lack of funds, or any other seeming lack, you can still be what you want to be and have what you want to have.

Yes, you can start right now without funds, without education, without friends or influence, without an idea, without anything but a sincere desire to be somebody expressing life, and you can be that person you have secretly always wanted to be, and you can have all the money you want to express yourself within every field of your own choosing.

Are you ready to put The Count to Four technique into action? I am sure that you are. I know that you are

How to Get Everything You Want - 19

because I know that you have many desires which you have never realized.

It has been said that 98 people out of every 100 have never decided just exactly what they want to be in life. That is, they have never come to any decision regarding a "life's goal" like Henry Ford, Thomas Edison or Andrew Carnegie. But here is the most important thing as far as I am concerned. It is understood that 98 out of every hundred haven't made that big decision, but I happen to know, and you do too, that you and I and every other person living at this moment has some desire, right at this moment, that we want to realize as soon as possible.

Ask yourself the question, "What do I want to be next?" "What do I want to attain next?" List all the things you want to be next and all the things you want to have next. Let's not worry too much about what we want next year or five years from now or 20 years from now, at this point. If you have just one little desire right now that you wish fulfilled and you don't know exactly how to go about it, then you are ready to learn how to "Count to Four".

Let's begin by looking at **Phase One** which is to i*dentify what you want.*

Write it down.

Define it.

Describe it.

There are several ways of helping your subconscious mind to become deeply impressed with exactly what you want. For example, you can cut pictures out of magazines and paste them in a scrapbook. If you can draw well, or if you know a friend who is an artist, you can create drawings or pictures of your idea of what you want.

By going through this simple mental process, your subconscious mind is impressed with exactly what you

How to Get Everything You Want - 20

want. I want to point out, right at this point, that what I am asking you to do does not cost you one red penny. I merely want you to do it so that we can cause your mind to go through certain "thoughts."

You see your thoughts as size and color and texture. One of the reasons a person is living a small, limited type of life now is that he is in the habit of thinking small, limited thoughts. So, for Phase One, *let's not ask the price.*

Let's just identify what we really want. It can be any size and color and texture and design. At this point, all we are concerned with is "a mental process" which does not cost a cent. So, do what I am asking you to do, because if you will, I guarantee you that you will realize your desire in every case.

So, with the humility of a little child, get yourself a notebook and write down everything that you want to be next and everything that you want to have next. First of all, just write them down in your own words so that you can read them and they will cause you to know what you want next.

Then, after you have written these things down, start cutting out the pictures which represent what you want and paste them in the notebook. For example, I have done this in regard to automobiles, and I have known many of my students to do the same. I decide that I want a certain automobile, then I write it down in my notebook. I go down to the dealer and obtain as many color pictures as possible and then I paste one of them in my notebook, on the wall by my bed, in the bathroom by the mirror and in my desk, so that every time I open the drawer I see the picture of what I want.

By doing all these things I accomplish the purpose of the ONE phase of of the formula of success. *I developed a keen, clear, distinct mental picture of exactly what I want.* The subconscious will help us obtain exactly what we want or if we give it a hazy, unclear, smeared concept or mental picture, it will help us obtain that.

Which would you rather have, just exactly what you want or a smeared, unclear approximation of what you want? I can tell you from hundreds of experiences that this works right down to a "T."

I might say here, that *of the thousands of successful people whom I have studied, every one of them had either consciously or unconsciously developed the ability to think distinctly and clearly, and to define and identify the things which they wanted.*

The millions of people who do not have the things they want, at the same time, have not developed their ability to think clearly. Yes, they had the same basic ability to learn to think distinctly as anybody, but they did not realize that it was important or that it had anything to do with him getting what they wanted, so they just continued to think in a blurred, indistinct manner.

When I found this out in my research I was deeply impressed and immediately started trying to think more clearly. I began to identify exactly what I wanted to be and have. I noticed right away, a change in my life. I had more of a feeling of harmony and peace as soon as I took charge of my thoughts and started to define distinctly what I wanted to be and have. Also, my financial situation began to get better and better.

Most of you will say at this point, "Well, I can certainly accomplish Phase One." As long as it doesn't cost anything, what have I got to lose? You say to yourself, "If there is just one remote possibility that this will work, even though I do not quite understand just how it works, I am certainly going to get started right away and obtain a nice notebook, and write down my secret dreams of what I

How to Get Everything You Want - 22

have always wanted to be and I am making a complete list of everything I want of a material nature.

"Since all he is asking me to do at this point, is to go through the mental activity, the least I can do is cooperate with him, as he promises me that I can be what I want to be and that I can have what I want to have. I am approaching this with just simple childlike faith as he has tested in his own life and many thousands of others and it has never failed.

"I don't have to understand just how it works, anymore than I have to understand the way my television set works in order to enjoy it fully; or anymore than I have to be an electrician in order to enjoy all the fine things which I enjoy through electricity. I must assume that there are 'laws' about which Dr. Jones is familiar, and he is sharing with me a simple little,one, two, three, four routine, which, if I follow, I can enjoy the full benefit of as though I understood it fully.

"I know that even little child can just turn on a light switch and not know anything about how it works, and all the lights will burn just as well for the child as if an expert electrician had turned on the light switch."

I must say just one more thing before I take you into the next phase which is Phase Two. I know that most of you will believe in this enough to try it. I congratulate you, because when you try it, you will find that it works.

And, of course, you will become what you want to be and you will have what you want to have. But there will be a few who think that they are so smart, that they will say, "Ah, that Jones guy is crazy." I would like to challenge you, if you should fall into this type.

Go ahead and prove me wrong. You can never honestly say that it won't work unless you try it and see whether it works or not. Go ahead, try it and prove me wrong. I have

How to Get Everything You Want - 23

a pleasant surprise for you. You will end up being what you want to be in having what you want to have.

Now, let's move to Phase Two.

Phase Two is also just a mental exercise, and it doesn't cost you one red penny. Phase Two is as follows: *"Pretend" that you already are what you want to be, and that you already have what you want to have.*

Ask yourself, "How would I feel if I were already the person I want to be? If I already had the things that I have written down on my Phase One list, how would I feel? What would I do? Where would I be right now?" In other words, assume the fulfilled dream.

Assume the feeling of the dream fulfilled. When a farmer plants a field of corn, he cultivates it, rains fall on it and the sun shines on it and it grows and grows until one day it is ready for the harvest. You see, Phase One of this formula is like planting the seed. Phase Two is like watering, cultivating and warming the soil by the sun shining on it. When you "pretend" that you are the person you want to be, you go through special mental activities or mental exercises which are like plowing the corn, or cultivating it.

When you assume the warm, deep emotional feeling of the person you want to be, it is like the warm sunshine shining on the growing corn. I can tell you many details of what actually takes place inside you and what happens in the whole universe, when you "pretend" but believe me, I know that if you will do it in simple childlike faith your dreams will come true. Is that fair enough at this point?

Later on, for those of you who are interested, I will be happy to go into the deeper aspects of the laws involved.

Someone will ask, "How do I comfortably go through these mental exercises of pretending that I am a certain

How to Get Everything You Want - 24

person in my dreams?"

One of the best ways that I have ever used is as follows:

1. I first assume that I have already attained my desire.
2. Then I ask myself what event would normally take place after I had attained my desire but would never take place other than if I had attained my desire.
3. Then I make arrangements to live that event as though I had already attained my desire.

For example, I went on the air on my first television program on June 19, 1955. I had my desire to be on television written down for several months before June, 1955. So, in March, 1955, I arranged an occasion to dramatize an event which would normally only take place after my first appearance on television. I arranged to have a debut party at my house, and the time was, as we pretend, the evening after I had debuted on TV that afternoon.

Each guest was invited and given a script, which told him exactly what to say at the party. So each guest arrived with great joy and enthusiasm congratulating me on having done a fine job that afternoon on my first telecast. All evening, our discussions were regarding how happy we all were that the program had been launched so well in the great good that would be done by the principles of genuine success being taken to so many hundreds of thousands of people, etc.

We pretend that we were celebrating the start of a television program in March, but the actual program did not start until June or about three months later. But we all assumed the mental attitude, the excited feeling, the tones of reality, of having already started the program. I happen

How to Get Everything You Want - 25

to know that by doing this very thing it played a very important part in bringing my dream into fulfillment so soon.

You don't have to do anything great in order to use this one, two, three, four technique.

Let's suppose that your little girl wants a new tricycle. One day you see her riding an old broom around in the backyard. You ask her what she is doing and she says, "I'm riding my new red tricycle." She is using the same technique. She, first of all, did Phase One, which is to decide that she wanted a new red tricycle; then she was doing Phase Two by riding the broom and pretending that it was already her actual new red tricycle. It's just that simple. It doesn't cost a penny so far, and it's just a mental activity which you go through like a little child.

Let's suppose that you want to be a person who has great poise so that you can meet all life situations without fear or feeling of nervousness. You would even like to be able to stand up and speak before groups with poison comfort. Then, if that is what you want, you have your Phase One part already.

What about Phase Two? You would do several things. Every time you attend a group meeting in the person of poise gets up and gives a really good speech, you see yourself as being the person giving that speech. Get that feeling of giving that speech by pretending that you are the person giving it. Also, give a party and coach your guests and celebrate your having given a great speech the day before. Also, line up some chairs in your living room, and one day when no one is there but you, assume that all those chairs are full of people.

Stand up and talk to them as long as you can think of anything to say. It doesn't matter at this point, just keep standing there and keep talking about anything whatsoever, and after a while you will get a feeling of comfort and you will then begin to control your thoughts. Then, after awhile, you will find yourself taking advantage of every opportunity of accepting appointments to speak before groups and you will one day find that you are a person of poise and confidence.

It doesn't matter whether you want to be the President of the United States, and Ambassador to a foreign country, a Congressman, a Senator, a movie star, a great singer, a great industrialist, a great attorney, a great salesman, a great farmer, a great housewife and mother, a great secretary, or a great whittler, you can become anything you want to be, big or little, by applying this one, two, three, four technique.

Can you fulfill Phase Two? Sure you can. All you need is the desire and humility of a little child.

But Phase Three is very important.

Phase Three is, *"That ability within you to say, Yes and No."*

Many people have not learned that it is their individual prerogative to evaluate any life situation or event or proposition and then down deep inside say, "Yes" if they believe it should be yes, and to say "No" if it should be no. I am not advising you whether, in certain circumstances, you should say "yes" or "no", but in order to emphasize this point, I would like to say that you have the power, and the right, and the ability, if you choose, to use it; and the God of Heaven gave you that power, right, and ability to use it.

Yes, you have within you the power, the right and the ability to look your father and mother right in the face and say "yes" or "no." You can look your minister right in the face and say "yes" or "no." You can look your husband, or your wife, right in the face and say "yes" or "no." You can

How to Get Everything You Want - 27

look your friend, or your so-called enemy in the face and say "yes" or "no." Yes, you can look even God in the face and say "yes" or "no", because he gave you "dominion" and that means that you can say "yes" or "no" to every source of suggestion, even your God, and face the possibility of enjoying the results of having made the right decision, or of suffering from having made the wrong decision.

But the point I am making is that you were given the right, the power, and the intelligence, and the ability to learn to say, "yes" or "no."

Now, you have followed the suggestions made in Phase One and Phase Two very closely. But, one day you will happen to mention what you are doing, to a friend, your husband or your wife, your mother or father, your minister, and one or more of them immediately begins to make fun of you or discourage you. They tell you, "You mean that you fell for that!"; "Don't be silly"; "I don't believe that stuff, and I think that you are nuts"; or some sort of discouragement.

Well, Phase Three of this technique is "down deep inside you." Pay no attention to them whatsoever, but keep your thoughts on Phase One and Phase Two. Keep identifying your desires, and keep "living in the feeling of having already attained them." *Yes, you can control your attention units. You can learn to say "no" to anything which will hinder the fulfillment of your dreams.* You are the master of your fate, the captain of your soul!

Again, let me stress that so far it doesn't cost anything. When I lecture on the subject around the country I consistently have people ask me, "How much does it cost me to quit being what I am now and become what I want to be? How much does it cost me to get the things I want now?"

How to Get Everything You Want - 28

Well, I tell them that I had discovered and have proved a simple little technique that really works every time. It is called the "IF YOU CAN COUNT TO FOUR TECHNIQUE" Phase One doesn't cost one cent. Phase Two doesn't cost a cent. And Phase Three doesn't cost a cent either. And now, let me tell you that Phase Four doesn't cost a cent either. Is that fair enough?

Phase Four is the *HOW!*

How do you get from here and now, to there, and what you want to be, and have what you want to have and not cost you anything?

Well, I am going to give you the answer in several ways so that you will be sure to trust it. First, let me say, that I am aware of certain facts, laws, rules, powers which are all natural, and which, if you will do certain things with the simple faith of a child, will all work for you and bring your dreams all fulfilled to you.

How many of you have ever had an idea come to you for "out of the blue?" All of you have, I am absolutely sure. Well, how many of you know just where the "blue" is located? I don't exactly know where it is located myself, but I know the name we give it.

The "blue" is your subconscious mind.

Now, your subconscious mind is like the "soil" into which the farmer plants seeds. The farmer plants for example, wheat. What grain does he expect to one day harvest? "Wheat, of course" you say. May I ask you "How does the farmer take one bushel of wheat, plant it in good soil and a few months later harvest, say 40 bushels? Where does the extra 39 bushels come from?" "Oh," you say, "Nature did it."

Well, the farmer has learned by experience that there is something, some power which he calls nature and that if he plants good seed in good soil in good season he can depend on this power in some manner or means which he does not completely understand to take his one bushel of wheat and increase it to 40 bushels.

At the same time, he knows this power does not steal this extra 39 bushels from the neighbor's granary. This power, in some fashion not fully understood takes just one bushel of seed, about an acre of soil, and about three or four months time.

The faith of the farmer, the warmth of the sun, the moisture of the rain, and other invisible elements, are combined and out of what appears to be "Nothingness" produces 40 new bushels of wheat. The farmer is pleased with the whole affair and his neighbor is not angry with him.

- Well, Phase One is the seed.
- Phase Two is the watering, cultivating, sunshine and faith.
- Phase Three is keeping the weeds out and not letting the enemy destroy your seed which has been well planted and is being cultivated until the harvest.
- Phase Four is the Subconscious Mind, which has the same quality in the field of LIFE as the soil has for the farmer.

In this way, the same as the soil takes one bushel of wheat and gives you forty fresh, new bushels of wheat, the subconscious takes one good idea, and through laws only known to itself, makes it into your dream fulfilled.

But you ask, "Just how are some of the ways that this all develops, or comes about in my daily life?"

I am glad to give you several examples.

How to Get Everything You Want - 30

Remember that you have done what it says to do in Phase One. Also, Phase Two and Phase Three. Now, there is a "period of time" that it takes the seed to germinate and the harvest to arrive in the form of your dream fulfilled. This all takes place quite naturally from day to day in your life. But each day you will have ideas come into your mind and you will do what these ideas suggest as they have to do with the progress toward the attainment of your desires.

For example, suppose that you want to enjoy the standard of living which requires an income of one thousand dollars per month. But right now, your income is only three hundred seventy-five dollars per month.

- Phase One, you identify your desire of an income of one thousand dollars per month.

- Phase Two, you pretend and feel as you think you would feel if you already had an income of a thousand per month.

- Phase Three, you would insist on maintaining that feeling regardless of any suggestion which would disagree with you.

- Phase Four, you would listen for an idea from your subconscious mind which will help you to actually earn and receive the thousand per month. One day, you ask a friend of yours, "How many ways are there in the world, which pay at least a thousand per month income?"

He tells you of over one hundred ways that pay at least that much. Your Subconscious Mind begins to function in a manner that it never has before. It begins to add things up for you. It tells you in the form of ideas, out of the "blue" and in the form of feelings and urges that you should begin to study in a certain field, perhaps attend a series of lectures, or read certain books, or attain the

How to Get Everything You Want - 31

necessary training to qualify for this new method which will permit you to earn and receive at least a thousand dollars per month. Of course, you not only listen to the subconscious, you do what it tells you to do.

You then, one day, find yourself in a new position that you enjoy very much and you are happier than you have ever been in your life. You are earning and receiving a thousand per month and your dream is a reality. The Count to Four Technique has worked for you and made it possible for you to almost triple your standard of living. It will help you to be anything you want to be and have anything you want to have.

Another example: A friend of mine is a man who, prior to three years ago, had never been in the direct selling field. He had been operating a modest dry cleaning business.

When I met him three years ago, he was a presser in a department store earning and receiving exactly $100 per week. He had never been before a group to make a talk at the time I met him. He had a 10th grade education, but like so many of us had not learned how to use the best of grammar as far as so-called correct speech was concerned. This man attended one of my lectures about three years ago, and he decided to do everything I asked him to do as I promised that he could be anything he wanted to be and that he could have anything he wanted to have.

In just three short years, he is a top sales executive of one of the most outstanding sales organizations in the world. His duties take him on lecture tours all over the United States, Canada, Hawaii and Alaska and soon he will go to Europe, Asia, Australia, New Zealand and Africa. He interviews the biggest people wherever he goes and his income is very substantial and is going up each year. He has everything he could desire. He lives in the finest suites at the finest hotels all over the world. He can do anything he desires because he has self confidence and an adequate amount of money.

Another example: About two years ago, I was lecturing along this line to a group of about 60 people near Los Angeles. Most of this small group were middle aged and older women in the selling field. I told them about the principles behind The Count to Four Technique. It was, as some of them told me later, just too good to be true. They wanted to believe it, but just found it impossible.

I felt this feeling among these very fine woman and I stopped right there on the spot and used The Count to Four Technique to help me to help them believe. I got the answer on the spot. I asked if there was at least one lady present, who is never, at any time, even secretly considered the idea of owning and casually driving a late model Cadillac automobile.

A charming lady raised her hand. In fact, several raised their hands, but I picked this one out as an example. I also asked her if she had an expensive dress. She said no, but that she would like one since I mentioned that she can have anything she wanted. Also, she said she was living in an apartment, which was very modest, that cost her about $30 per month. She was driving a used compact car, which at the time was worth about three-hundred and seventy-five dollars. I think that you all can get the picture.

Now, I told the group that in six months or less, this lady would own and be driving a late model Cadillac, be wearing a new expensive knit dress, and would be living in a new and expensive apartment comparable to her new way of life. They all looked goggle-eyed at me as though to say, "Can this really be true or is he a fool?"

Not six months later, but just 5 and one-half weeks later, this lady had her late model Cadillac, her knit dress and her new apartment. And all that she did was use what I

How to Get Everything You Want - 33

have asked you to do in The Count to Four Technique.

She got well long into the plan, and after a week or so her subconscious mind began asking, "How can I earn and receive more money, because now I am a Cadillac girl and not a second-hand compact car girl. I'm a knit dress girl now, and I am a girl who lives in a new expensive apartment with period furniture. I want to find a way so I can be of greater service to humanity so that I can receive more compensation so I can comfortably live by my new standard."

Well, this lady's self-confidence and her sales increased so that she jumped from where she was at the time of the first lecture, to where she was just 5 and one-half weeks later. That has been a little less than two years ago, and now, I still know this very nice lady and at this time she is looking at a brand-new Cadillac. By the way, along with all the things which I mentioned, she also grew in poise, self-confidence, charm, patience, love of service, generosity, and many other very desirable mental attributes.

Her income today is at least three times what it was two years ago. Her self-confidence is 10 times what it was two years ago, and all because she decided to let me experiment in her case. She did not know exactly how it was going to happen, but she had confidence in me and did just exactly what I asked her to do. You say, "Yeah, he tells us these things, but he doesn't give us their names and addresses." If all you need, to believe this enough to try it, is to be able to contact this lady and ask her if I am telling you the truth, I'll be happy to give you names and addresses.

The way to state the Phase Four principle is this:

The size and color of your thoughts are cause. Your experiences are effect.

Each thought has size and color or quality and quantity.

How to Get Everything You Want - 34

Your thought regarding income is cause. Your income is effect.

If you could go through some sort of mental exercise and thereby increase the quality and quantity of your thought, which is cause, soon the income, which is effect, would be increased accordingly.

The Count to Four Technique is a mental exercise, which expands our thoughts regarding our desires and the law of cause and effect brings our desires to pass.

You ask Mr. A. how much his income is at present, and he tells you that it is $400 per month. You ask him what kind of a house he lives in, and he tells you he lives in a $75 per month house. You ask him why he doesn't live in a $200 per month house, on a $400 per month income.

Let's assume that he wants, very much, to live in a certain house which he can obtain for $200 per month. Let's now further assume that he goes to night school and gets a new job, where his services are now worth $650 per month instead of $400 per month. Now he obtains the $200 per month house and lives in it.

How much does it cost him? We will all have to admit that all he did was to increase the quality and quantity of his "thoughts" and this resulted in his 40 hours per week being worth $650 per month instead of the $400 earned previously. So, it didn't cost him anything to move into the $200 per month house from the $75 per month house.

Please try to think this through until it really means something to you. I know men who used to work very hard for $400 per month.

They worked hard for over 40 hours per week. Now they have so increased the value of their services per hour, that they work fewer hours, expand less energy and they are

How to Get Everything You Want - 35

earning and receiving $4000 per month. I can take any man or woman, regardless of station in life, and if they will follow The Count to Four Technique, they can increase the quality and quantity of their "thoughts" and thereby increase the value of their services.

In turn, they will increase the amount of their income, and they can then obtain what they want. The Count to Four Technique will work for you regardless of whether your present income is $20 per week or $2000 per week. It is a principle which will make it possible for anyone, in any station in life, to merely decide what he wants to be and to have and then become it and have it.

It is now time that every person in the whole world should be told that success is just as simple as one, two, three, four. It is not as complicated as we have been told for centuries. It is good to get a formal education and to know as much as you can.

We have been told, however, that an education is indispensable and absolutely necessary before one can be successful. That is not so.

"If you can count to four", you can be anything you want to be and can have anything you want to have.

I know this to be true, and I challenge anyone to prove me wrong!

BONUS

Get Related Materials
from Our Free Library
Instant Access – Join Here

Click or type into your browser:

http://livesensical.com/go/freelibrary/

Printed in Great Britain
by Amazon